Victorian and Edwardian
NOTTINGHAMSHIRE
from old photographs

Victorian and Edwardian
NOTTINGHAMSHIRE
from old photographs

Introduction and commentaries by
SHEILA M. COOKE

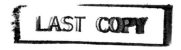
B. T. BATSFORD LTD
LONDON

First published 1976
Text copyright © Sheila Cooke 1976
Filmset by Servis Filmsetting, Manchester
Printed by The Anchor Press, Tiptree
for the Publishers B. T. Batsford Ltd
4 Fitzhardinge Street, London W1H 0AH

ISBN 0 7134 3116 4

CONTENTS

ACKNOWLEDGMENTS

The author wishes to thank the following people for advice and informatio
Mr R. Baker, Mr S. Best, Mr G. Dickinson, Miss E. Hadfield, Mrs P. Heathco
Mr A. Henstock, Mr K. Negus, Mr H. V. Radcliffe, Miss J. Sims, Mr K. Trai
Mr A. D., Mrs E. M. and Miss H. Uppadine and Mr R. Venner.

Photographs are reproduced by permission of the Nottinghamshire Coun
Council with the exception of the following:
nos 114, 115 the family of Albert R. Atkey; 104 B.P.B. Industries Ltd; 1, 7, 34, 3
51, 57, 65, 66, 69, 70, 90, 92, 95, 138, 141 the family of Arthur Hudson; 44, 61, 8
121, 124, 137 Newark District Council's Museum; 79, 97, 125, 128 Ruddingt
Village Museum.

INTRODUCTION

The first commercial photographer in Nottinghamshire was John Frederick Davis, formerly a portrait painter, who established a studio in Bromley House on Angel Row, Nottingham about 1850. His photographic institution advertised 'life in portraiture with certainty and accuracy in all except foggy weather'. He moved ten years later to another studio in Albert Street where his successor, Samuel Kirk, was patronised by the Prince of Wales and gained many exclusive commissions from local societies and organisations. In 1853 many photographic patents were relaxed, leading to an increase in the numbers of professional photographists, as they were termed in the trade directories. By 1858 seventeen Nottingham men were offering their newly acquired skills to the public. They were joined four years later by an American, Alonzo G. Grant, who boasted fifteen years experience in New York and London. He opened a large photographic and fine art gallery in Long Row using chemicals and apparatus imported from the United States. He offered fast, efficient processing – orders received before mid-day were ready for collection the following afternoon. Mr Grant's varied services included the loan of stereoscopic slides for private parties, producing duplicates of Daguerreotypes often superior to the originals and giving 'hints on the production of good negatives (gratis) to professionals who favoured him with their finishing'. His assistants, who were 'especially adapted by long experience to the various branches' of the business, printed work for amateurs and took 'pleasing and truthful' portraits of infants, invalids and deceased persons at the shortest notice. The firm's charges were very reasonable: album portraits cost 4 shillings for four, a paper portrait by the negative process cost 5 shillings while that from a glass negative only 7 shillings coloured, a charge of one half extra being made for each additional person in the picture. The finished prints were touched up and tinted with oil, watercolours and india ink.

Alfred Cox moved into Davis's vacant studio in Bromley House. A carver and gilder before establishing his photographic business, Cox was the first to introduce *cartes-de-visite* portraits into the town. These paper prints pasted onto mounts similar in size to a visiting card were patented in France in 1854. They were relatively cheap, at one shilling each within the range of the ordinary person and therefore extremely popular.

The main importer and dealer in photographic apparatus and materials in the town was J. Shepperley of Long Row. An advertisement for his shop in 1858 gives some idea of the processes used in the town at that time. Mr Shepperley stocked superior negative and positive collodion and the albumenized paper used in the collodion or wet plate process. A glass negative producing a positive, normally on albumen paper, was a method introduced in 1851 and used almost exclusively by photographers until the 1870s. Two other features of the advertisement are the stereoscopic cameras and views. Two almost identical paper prints mounted side by side on card give a three-dimensional picture when viewed through a stereoscope. One London firm was offering over 100,000 different views for sale at between one shilling and one shilling and sixpence each. The photograph of the Gateway School, Clipstone (Fig 43), is one half of a stereoscopic card.

The Mr Cox who introduced *cartes-de-visite* to Nottingham is also to be thanked for training some of the County's best photographers of the later Victorian period. One of the most successful of his pupils was Henri Louis Morel whose patrons included the leading families of the County within a few years of setting up business in 1886. This was hardly surprising as the premises in Newcastle Chambers, apart from his own private suite, developing, printing and toning rooms, offered the public four handsomely furnished reception and dressing rooms. During the summer months a stream of water flowed over the glass roof of the studio, keeping the air cool and the light pure. His reputation, however, was built on the quality of his work, which embraced indoor and outdoor, landscape, equestrian, architectural and engineering photography. Every new process or improvement was utilised by him as soon as it became available and the public described his work as art.

Another important member of the profession at this time was Joseph Byron. Between 1879 and 1889 Joseph worked in a succession of Nottingham studios, having been taught by his father, James, in business since 1862. Joseph Byron emigrated to New York about 1890, where he continued in the profession with great success. His photograph of the tug-o-war at Welbeck Abbey is from a small collection of his local work which was sent back to England by his descendants.

An interesting selection of prints taken from negatives which passed through the hands of another local firm is preserved in an album compiled by Henry Edward Bird, whose studio was at St Peter's Church Walk, Nottingham. The range of work he received is very wide and includes Nottingham street scenes and events, views of the county, family snapshots and holiday photographs from places as far afield as Edinburgh and Cheltenham. Most of his own work was portrait photography and some of this, delicately hand-coloured, has also survived.

In 1890 Mr Ephraim Short of Britannia Chambers, Pelham Street was popularizing platinotypes. This process, which utilised platinum for coating the print in place of silver salts was patented in 1873. It enabled Mr Short to produce permanent and artistic photographs, as platinum prints have delicate half tones and a soft silver-grey appearance. The subject of his portrait was gracefully posed in front of scenery or surrounded by artistic drapery. Clever effects of light and shade, together with the studio props, enabled Mr Short to compose a good picture as well as an accurate portrait. Skilled artists were employed to finish the work in crayon, oil or water-colour, arts considered necessary to produce work which would be acceptable to the paying customer.

The increase in the numbers of professional photographers was matched by the growing interest of amateurs. In Nottinghamshire this resulted in the formation of the Nottingham Photographic Society. In January 1859 the Society held a conversazione and exhibition in the Exchange Rooms. At the same time a large exhibition was mounted of materials and equipment which included a solar camera, tripod stands, a dark tent, microscopes, lenses and an amazing photograph of a £20 note' by Mr Thompson, an optician. The photographs by members remained on show for a week at a small charge to the public. The judging for the prizes was performed by George Shadholt of Middlesex, who was asked to take into account 'the various qualities, including artistic composition, and without reference to the process, which characterise excellency in photography'. He found these rules easy to apply in class C, the stereoscopic views. Fifty seven were submitted and the prize was awarded to one of Mr Woodward's six specimens. His views, including two of Wilford Village and Peterborough Cathedral had both artistic merit and technical excellence. Of the five entries in class B for small-size prints it was also easy to award the prize to Mr Hurley for a view of Newark Castle. In class A, however, Mr Shadholt found himself in a dilemma. There were only eight photographs in the section for prints of 10" × 8" or larger. A calotype of Southwell Minster by the Rev. Mr Dredge was very artistic in treatment, but taken by an imperfect lens which distorted the angles of the building. The calotype process, which used a paper negative, could not record fine detail and the faults of the print were therefore inherent in the process itself. The other contender for the prize was a faultless print from a glass negative by Samuel Bourne, showing Regent Street, Nottingham. His equipment was excellent, a very good lens reproducing exact proportions and perfect angles. The judge considered, however, that so much skill applied to a mere street scene of very little architectural merit and totally destitute of every vestige of life was labour thrown away. The Society awarded the prize to the Rev. Dredge, voting for artistic merit rather than technical quality.

The Rev. Mr Dredge, therefore, had his moment of glory, but it was Samuel Bourne who went on to make a lasting and nationally acknowledged contribution to photography. Born in Staffordshire in 1834, Samuel moved early in life to Nottingham to work in Moore and Robinson's Bank. Taking up photography at the age of twenty he recorded views in Nottinghamshire and Derbyshire before going to India in 1863. Here he established the firm of Bourne and Shepherd in Calcutta, Simla and Bombay. In 1866 he made one of his three photographic journeys in India through the higher Himalayas. Three albums of these photographs, forming only part of a collection of nearly 1,600, were treasured by his family and recently deposited in a photographic library. Returning from his first visit to India he married Margaret, the daughter of Abraham Tolley and on his final return to England in 1869 he went into partnership with his wife's brother as a cotton doubler. 'Bright lands', the house built for him in the Park, Nottingham, in 1887 included a photographic room and a studio. Mr Bourne, a Unitarian and Justice of the Peace, took up painting in later life, becoming President of the Nottingham Society of Artists. His paintings of woodland and river scenery were influenced by his work in photography being detailed and picturesque. He died in 1912, a respected member of the community.

An amateur photographer whose work is represented frequently in this volume is Arthur Hudson, who was born in 1876 and raised by an Uncle and Aunt, his parents having died when he was young. Early in this century he was the Mansfield reporter for the *Nottingham Daily Express* and *Evening News,* working from his office on Queen Street and his home on Redcliffe Road. Many hundreds of his half-plate glass negatives are preserved by his family. The subjects range from views of the Mansfield and Sutton area to those of Derbyshire, the Lincolnshire coast and some of Germany. The collection, which includes many family portraits, both formal groups and scenes of daily life, is one of the finest in the county.

1 A photographer's stall at Goose Fair. George Hickling, in his poem *The Fair,*
Here your portrait is taken, and here you are weighed,
and here try your strength if a penny is paid
refers to portrait photography at Goose Fair in 1861

2 Mr H. E. Bird, third from left, an amateur photographer, with members of his family 19 April 1888

3 The Bourne family posed in the garden in 1860 shortly before Samuel left for India

4 Children on swings from H. E. Bird's photograph album. He marked it 'instantaneous plate'

5 The reception room at Mr Ephraim Short's Studio on Pelham Street, Nottingham in 1892

6 Mr and Mrs Joseph Byron and Mr and Mrs George Caldwell, Nottingham photographers, at the Duke of Portland's garden party at Welbeck Abbey in 1899

7 Arthur Hudson on the steps of the
rock houses near his home in Mansfield

STATIONS
MARKET PLACE
SHERWOOD

EMPIRE · PYATTS
THE FANCY DRAPERS

SHERWOOD

5

43328. Nottingham

TOWNS AND
VILLAGES

8 *previous page* Nottingham extended its boundaries in 1877 to take in many of the surrounding villages. This fact, coupled with the thriving textile industries, helped to increase the population from 53,000 in 1841 to 260,000 only seventy years later. This view shows the North-east corner of the Market Place and Long Row in 1902. In the centre is the now demolished Black Boy Hotel, its façade designed in 1893 by one of the city's most famous Victorian architects, Watson Fothergill. On the right is the corner of the Exchange Buildings occupied by Beecrofts toy shop, and on the left is the cross-city tram about to turn into Queen Street. This service began in October 1901, charging a fare of 2d from the Market Place to Sherwood

9 Bestwood Road, Papplewick in 1886. The population of just over three hundred were mainly farm workers. Near the lodge of Papplewick Hall is the cave known as Robin Hood's Stable

10 The terminus of the tram from Mansfield outside the Methodist church in Sutton Road, Hucknall Huthwaite in 1907. Trams were replaced by motor buses in 1932. The principal occupations of the town were hosiery and coal mining

11 Westgate, Mansfield in 1908. On the left is number five, the premises of John Linney, printer and proprietor since 1870 of the *Mansfield and North Notts. Advertiser* and William Linney, bookseller, stationer, steam printer, wholesale newsagent and owner of a paperhanging warehouse

12 East Bridgford is a village on the Fosse Way near the site of Margidunum, a Roman military station. All the children in the neighbourhood must have gathered for the photographer of this postcard in 1907

13 Plumtree is a farming village in the south of the county. The population of 230 was served by two public houses in 1907 both run by local farmers. This is the Farmers Arms, the other was the Griffin

14 The entrance to Outram Street, Sutton-in-Ashfield in 1870, at that time known as Tenter Lane, from Forest Street. The cottages stand on the site later occupied by the gas works. Before the Local Board made up the road, stepping stones had to be used to walk over the mud. On the right are the works of Messrs Jarvis, stone masons

15 Southwell has been a Cathedral town since 1884. In the centre of the photograph are the Assembly Rooms built in 1805. The carriage is standing outside the Saracen's Head Hotel, posting house and parcels office. It was here that Charles I surrendered to the Scots in May 1646

16 A row of cottages in Barton-in-Fabis, a farming village on the Trent with such a small population that the wheelwright ran the Post Office and the dairyman was also a carrier to Nottingham

17 Retford is a market town in the north of the county. At the turn of the century large quantities of the produce from the local villages supplied Sheffield via the Saturday markets. This photograph shows the Market Square. The Doric cast iron pillar and pedestal in the centre is twenty two feet high and was erected in 1831 to hold five gas lamps. In the centre distance is the red brick and Bath stone Wesleyan Methodist Church in Grove Street built in 1880 on the site of a previous chapel at a cost of £5,000

8 The ancient borough of Newark, a Royalist stronghold in the Civil War, contains many historic buildings including the beautiful church of St Mary Magdalene. The principal trade was in malt and flour, but brewing, iron and brass founding, gypsum mining and various light engineering works also provided employment in the town. This postcard by Francis Frith shows Bridge Street leading into the Market Place in the background. On the right a cart stands outside George Clutterbuck's butcher shop and the Wing Tavern. On the left are the Home and Colonial Stores and Freeman, Hardy and Willis, bootmakers, at number twelve

THE RICH AND THE POOR

19 In 1877 these faithful servants had completed a total of nearly two hundred years of service with Colonel Samuel and Mrs Welfit of Langwith Lodge, Cuckney: Mr Hubbard, butler, John Marsh, coachman, Henry Flint, bailiff, John Tomlins, gardener, Thomas Booth, keeper, William Whitehead, under-gardener

20 The farm workers of Scarrington built the hamlet of Little Lunnon. Walls were made of mud and roofs thatched with stubble from the fields. The sixteen two-room cottages had no sanitation and water was drawn from a communal well only seven feet deep

21 This postcard was being sent by Whatton residents only weeks after lightning struck the house on 29 March 1904. The destruction reveals walls only one brick thick and the straw used in the ceiling plaster

22 King Edward and his party as-
sembled in front of Rufford Abbey, the
home of their host, Lord Savile, on
9 September 1904 for this official
photograph. Later that morning the
Royal party attended the Doncaster
races, travelling by train from Ollerton
station. The previous day, after a
morning of croquet, the King had
visited Welbeck in the Royal Mercedes

23 The tropical house at Welbeck
Abbey was one of the many building
and improvement projects of the 5th
Duke of Portland. This eccentric recluse
spent £100,000 per year for eighteen
years on his estates

Royal Group, Rufford Abbey. 1904.

24 A fashionably dressed lady pays a duty visit to the poorer part of Barton village. Two of the women have been hoeing root crops in the fields, one of the few agricultural jobs performed by women

25 The complete population of the hamlet of Sutton Woodhouse in working clothes. The older women wear the traditional bonnet and shawl

26 Pendock Neale turned Tollerton Hall into a sham castle in the late eighteenth century. The photograph shows the hatchment of Mrs Susannah Davies who died in November 1872, having been lady of the manor for more than twenty years

THE CHURCH

27 Saint Barnabas Roman Catholic Cathedral on Derby Road, Nottingham replaced a chapel in George Street. Said to be Augustus Pugin's finest English church, it was opened in 1844 and formed the centre of the new Nottingham Diocese in September 1850

DERBY ROAD, NOTTINGHAM

28 The Navvy Mission Society, founded in Yorkshire in the 1870s, erected this mission room on Main Street, Bulwell to serve those men working on the Great Central line in 1898

29 The Sunday School demonstrations in Arnold took place on Whit Tuesday. In 1906 more than 4000 children marched from the schools to the football field to sing hymns. After the return procession around the town they had tea and played games

30 The Temperance Movement began in Nottinghamshire in the 1850s. The Hucknall Band of Hope persuaded societies not to meet in public houses and started a penny bank. On 13 June 1896 the President, the Duchess of Portland, entertained 750 of the members at Welbeck

31 Members of the choir gather in the Primitive Methodist Chapel at Keyworth on Easter Monday 1900. The chapel, built in 1828, held over two hundred people

32 The Ossington coffee tavern on Beastmarket Hill in Newark was opened in 1882 as a temperance establishment. It was built at a cost of £25,000 by Charlotte, Viscountess Ossington and included a coffee room, ladies room, billiard room and bedrooms for travellers. Outside the gardens were laid out for tea in summer and included a skittle alley. It became a favourite resort for cyclists

33 Seated at the organ of Saint Lawrence's Church, Gotham is the wife of the Rector, Frederick Armine Woodhouse, who was also Rural Dean of West Bingham and Vicar of Ratcliffe-on-Soar

DAILY LIFE

34 Arthur Hudson took this photograph of his wife Sarah Ellen doing the family wash in her scullery at 62, Redcliffe Road, Mansfield c.1905. She is using the ponch to clean the clothes in the dolly tub which she fills from the copper in the corner

35 Children in their Sunday clothes walking along Main Street, Sutton Bonington, pass in front of the Gables Farm

36 Children playing in a Mansfield back yard on washday wear pinafores similar to those on the line, to protect their dresses. *c.*1905

57 The hearse carrying Matilda Lambert enters Redhill cemetery. She and her three children were killed by Samuel Atherley, an Arnold labourer, at their house in Robinson's Yard in July 1909. Atherley was executed in Bagthorpe Gaol in December

58 The Society wedding of Hylda Sophia Paget and W. A. Tilney took place on 18 December 1902 at Saint Michael's church, Sutton Bonington. Here the bridesmaids, Lady Osborne and Misses Ashton, King-Hall, Yearsley, Constable and Packe are arriving at the church dressed in cream voile and lace

39 The houses excavated from sandstone at the top of Ratcliffe Gate, Mansfield are first mentioned in 1790 but are much older. By 1894 only one was occupied by a Mr Bramwell, who turned the former stackyards of the besom makers into a garden

EDUCATION

40 Seven pupils of the Lilley and Stone Girls High School, Newark in 1890. Although hand spinning became unprofitable about 1820, scholars were still obliged to spend half their time spinning while the remainder was devoted to singing, needlework, English grammar and religious knowledge. The present school in London Road was built in 1910

41/42 Samuel Brunts of Mansfield founded a charity in 1709 'for putting to school poor boys and making them fit for an honest trade.' Part of this endowment and the whole of a bequest by Charles Thompson was used to establish the Brunts Technical School. Designed by Messrs Evans and Jolly, it was built at a cost of £6000 and opened by Lord Belper in July 1894. The number of pupils rose from 75 initially to 190 in 1900. On the right is the workshop as it was in 1900, and below the physics laboratory in 1908

43 In 1895 an average of thirty pupils attended the Archway Lodge School at Clipstone. Education and clothing were provided by the Duke of Portland for poor girls of the parish aged five to fifteen and boys aged five to seven

44 The Grammar School at Newark was founded by Thomas Magnus in 1532. The new building, which cost £16,000 including furniture, was opened by Lord Belper in May 1909

45 Arnold British School was erected in 1868 for 268 boys and 250 infants. Miss Sarah Boulton, the infants' mistress, stands beside a class of the 1890s. The size of this class and the general appearance of the children contrasts sharply with that shown in the photograph of Carlton School (overleaf)

46 *overleaf* Carlton National School on Main Street was built in 1869. This infants class in 1902 was posed more imaginatively than was usual in an official school photograph

PUBLIC SERVICES

47 Newark fire station on Portland Street was erected in 1890 at a cost of £1000. The equipment included a telescopic fire escape, one manual and one steam engine and two reels of hose

48 Thomas Harrison, the captain, and his men proudly display the challenge cup that the brigade won on 25 July 1899

49 Front Street police station at Arnold was one of ten serjeants' stations in the Nottingham Division of the county constabulary. The photograph shows Robert Bones Hornsey, resident serjeant, and seven constables in 1892. Constables were expected to be 'bold in action, have a perfect command of temper, keep their boots and belts polished and never to carry an umbrella on duty'

The Robin Hood Rifles, marching
Bulcote in 1907, were formed in 1859
wing to the fear of invasion by
apoleon III. The battalions served in
e Boer War and on 1 April 1908 the
giment became the 7th Battalion, the
herwood Foresters

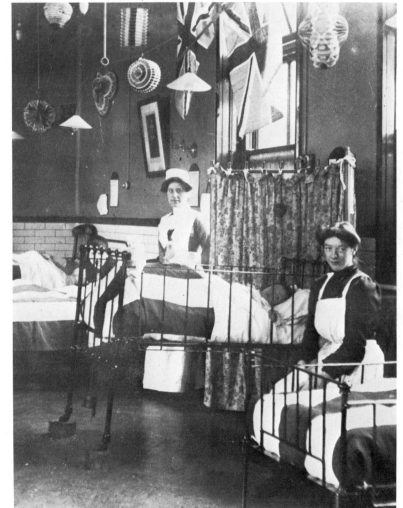

Mansfield's hospital, for accident
ses only, was moved to Union Street
1887 and enlarged in commemora-
on of Queen Victoria's Diamond Jubi-
e. Four medical officers and the
atron, Miss Florence Ransford, tended
atients in the hospital's sixteen beds

52 Nottingham received water from five well sites. This one at Burton Joyce, first used in 1898, was extended in 1908. The boreholes were sunk about 500 feet into the bunter sandstone beds, the water coming to the surface under pressure from a partial artesian supply

53 These street cleaners at Radcliffe-on-Trent used a cart belonging to a local builder, William Vickerstaff. Photograph c.1900

TRANSPORT

54 Horse and driver look equally cold and miserable as their cab travels up Beastmarket Hill, Nottingham in 1909. (In the background are the premises of Truman's, wine and spirit merchants)

55 Edward Mann, originally a cab proprietor and livery stable owner, ran this horse bus to West Bridgford from St Peter's Square, Nottingham, every half hour. When the licence for the service was withdrawn in 1914 the driver became a conductor on a Nottingham Corporation Transport bus

56 The Ruddington Carrying Society ran an omnibus to the Black's Head in Broad Marsh, Nottingham daily. The fare was only 4d when this photograph was taken in 1898

57 Arthur Hudson's family set out on a jaunt in a hired brake c.1905. It stands outside his home at 62, Redcliffe Road, Mansfield

58 John Wilson, a Sutton-in-Ashfield carter, with his removal van outside the vicarage. c.1910

59 The Dog and Gun on Trinity Street was the base of the carriers to villages north of Nottingham. Some of the carts are here lined up in the square alongside Holy Trinity church; Samuel Wyld, carter to Redhill and Calverton every other weekday and Saturdays at 4 p.m., Smith of Farnsfield and Ollerton, Gibson to Oxton and Dunthorne to Woodborough

60 The toll bar and weighing machine houses at Sutton Woodhouse. The keeper, Mrs Shore, is sitting in the foreground. The tolls of 1½d for a horse, 3d for a horse and cart etc., collected from three bars in the town paid for the upkeep of Sutton's roads until the gates were removed in 1872

61 David Hoe ran the Royal Oak posting house at North Collingham in 1894. He offered livery stables, hunters and carriages for hire and provided luncheons and dinners for commercials or pleasure parties

62 The Trent Navigation Company was formed in 1783 and started carrying in 1887. Goods to and from Hull, Gainsborough and Newark were transported in fourteen-foot wide barges and unloaded at the Company's Island Street wharf in Nottingham. Goods for Birmingham and Leicester were transhipped here to narrow boats belonging to Fellows, Morton and Clayton. The wharves were on the Nottingham Canal, which, together with the Beeston cut, forms the navigable by-pass to the river through the City

63 One of the lesser-known of the ten or so ferries over the River Trent, operated in 1900 by Henry Upton, crossed from Radcliffe to Carlton. The church registers record many drownings resulting from attempted horseback crossings of the old ford

64 A barge of the Trent Navigation Company

5 The Mansfield and District Light Railway Company ran their first tram on 11 July 1905 from the Market Place to Pleasley. This tram passes under the railway arches on its return journey from Berry Hill Lane to the Market Place

66 Sutton Junction station on the Kirkby to Mansfield line was opened in October 1849. The six-sailed tower mill, now demolished, had eight floors

67 In 1847 the Midland Railway laid two and a half miles of single track to Southwell as a branch from the Nottingham to Newark line. The track was doubled and extended to Mansfield in the 1870s. By 1900 two or three trains ran through the station each day, a vast improvement in the service since 1853 when the weekly train was horse drawn! The railwayman standing on the up line is shunting

68 Towards the end of the railway boom many old houses and shops, covering an area of thirteen acres, were demolished to enable the Great Central and Great Northern railways to build a joint station in Nottingham at a cost of over one million pounds. 600,000 cubic yards of material, mainly sandstone, were excavated during 1898 and 1899. The station was opened in May 1900 and named Victoria one month later

69/70 The early automobilist wanted to race. The first successful speed trials in Britain took place at Welbeck as part of the 1000 mile trial in May 1900. In succeeding years the Nottingham Automobile Club organised meetings on the Duke of Portland's private track, Clipstone Drive

71 Alfred Lewis, the Cotgrave carrier who ran a service to Nottingham on Wednesdays and Saturdays, soon realised the possibilities of the internal combustion engine. He expanded his business to found Lewis's Motors Limited, a small omnibus company. The extremely robust wheels are chain driven. *c.*1910

AGRICULTURE

72 Hucknall Mill, Sandy Lane, was bought in 1795 by the Windmill or Sick Club, a mutual aid society of artisans. It was moved from Broomhill when trees obstructed the original site. In the lane are 'Little Charlie' Rumbelow, the local joiner and undertaker, and his wife. Flower shows were held in the field on the left

73 Whatton-in-the-Vale tower mill in 1895. At the entrance are John Frederick and Jasper Houghton, the miller and his son. Many years later, as a result of an argument between them, the old man fell to his death from the fantail

74/75 In the north of the county the strong loam of the Keuper marl areas provides perfect soil for the production of celery, strawberries, raspberries, cherries, plums and apples. The two photographs show apple picking by hired labourers and strawberry gathering by a charabanc party at John Parr's farm at North Wheatley in 1900

76 Scarrington's farm labourers travel to church for the harvest festival on a Lincolnshire waggon decorated with corn, flowers and a plough

77   George Brown, one of the labourers
at Edward Shaw's farm, Main Street,
Keyworth, sitting outside the side door
of the house in 1900

78 This timber drag belongs to Godley and Goulding, timber merchants of Eastgate, Worksop. This town maintained a large trade in timber sawing, windsor chairs and wooden packing cases for Sheffield cutlery

79 A traction engine with a removable extension chimney, capped with a spark arrester, supplies the power for log sawing at a farm in Distillery Street, Ruddington: possibly that of Thomas Osinbrook

80 M. Starbuck and C. Green in the stackyard of Porchester Farm, Bingham. By 1900 young men were labouring on farms for the few years necessary to obtain a good reference and then leaving for more lucrative jobs in the towns. The average wage of the farm labourer was £1 per week and the use of a cottage

81/82 Haymaking in Clifton meadows in 1895 was hard work for the horses pulling the mowing machine and hay waggon and for the men scything and pitching the hay. Only the children are at leisure to enjoy the wonderful smell and the fine weather

83 Eel fishing in the River Trent, noted in the Domesday Book in 1085, is here practiced over 800 years later at Colwick. Mature, or silver, eels are netted during the journey down river, the first stage of their migration to the breeding grounds

84 Rick building at Saxondale in 1896. The single cylinder traction engine would have cost about £500. Most of Saxondale's eight five inhabitants were farmers and farm workers

85 The result of a badger hunt in 1908 on the Earl of Caernarvon's estate near Shelford

86 A horse-drawn harrow breaks down the seed bed into a fine tilth in the fields below the derelict post mill at Ravensdale near Mansfield

CRAFTS

87 These rod peelers are working in the osier beds or rod holts at Fiskerton. The finished willow rods were probably sold to the basket weavers at Sutton-on-Trent, who paid £20 per ton

88 Beany Chapell was Norwell's odd job man, living on Mount Pleasant, Bathley Road for many years. He boasted of having been outside England only once – when he visited Derbyshire!

89 John Henry Shumach, naturalist and taxidermist, in his workshop in Church Street, Southwell in 1895. His home was in Easthorpe and for some years he was deputy registrar of births and deaths for the Southwell district

90 John Beighton, blacksmith, of Red Lion Court, Mansfield holds the handle of the bellows in his smithy 1900–1905

91 Francis and Thomas Peberdy, farriers and smiths, shoeing outside the smithy at Normanton-on-Soar in 1890

92 An old lady in the Mansfield area spinning. Her left hand guides the thread from the distaff onto the spindle, which is rotated by the cord encircling the large wheel which she turns with her right hand

93 The saddler at Keyworth until his
death in 1906 was John Henry Pickard.
The photograph shows him at the door
of his shop in Main Street sewing
leather firmly held in a knee vice

94 John Kelk outside his workshop in Kilton Road, Worksop in 1904. His main trade was chair making and six Windsor chairs with decorative splats stand beside cricket bats in various stages of completion, the product of his other skill

INDUSTRIES

95 This frame-work-knitters work-shop in the Mansfield area in 1900 has windows extending the whole length of the room to admit the maximum amount of natural light. Although only three frames are visible, there would have been six or seven in the workshop

96 In 1798 Hezekiah Clark established a company at Retford for the dying and finishing of cloth. This machine was designed by the firm's own engineers in 1900. The girls are using steam bolts to finish the fancy work on sleeves

97 Many of the women of Ruddington were lace workers. This photograph of lace menders was taken outside the shop of John Mee in Kirk Lane. Lace manufacture is a leisure industry subject to great fluctuations mirroring the prosperity of the country. Consequently the fortunes of lace workers could change from prosperity to poverty within the space of ten years

98 The stocking frame was invented by William Lee of Calverton in 1589. In 1844 over 1600 frames were worked by knitters in the County, usually in their own homes. More than half the population of Ruddington was involved in various branches of the hosiery industry in 1850 and it was still the principal employment in 1900, when this photograph of frame-work knitters was taken, although by then the frames were often grouped in small factories and workshops

99 A miner waits in one of the pit cages at the bottom of number two shaft in Clifton colliery in 1895. The winding engine will soon draw this cage up to the surface as the other descends guided by four wire ropes. The foul air from the mine was also drawn out through this shaft

100 *previous page* Boys as well as men were employed above ground in the screens where they picked stone from the coal. After falling from the moving belt in the foreground the coal is sorted into sizes ready for sale. Clifton colliery closed in 1969

101 Loaded coal tubs stand at the entrance to number one shaft where 'Arthur', the winding engine, will haul them from the mine. Fresh air for the pit was drawn in through the same shaft, in winter chilling to the bone those miners checking the loads at the bottom

102 Clifton colliery, which was sunk in 1868, had an underground workshop for making and capping the wire haulage ropes. A large pipe removes smoke and fumes from the furnace on the left

103 The Bolsover Colliery Company had been established fifteen years before it sank the Crown Farm colliery at Mansfield in 1904. To house the miners the Company built Forest Town, a model village of 320 tied dwellings. These were constructed in numbered avenues, each house with a yard and garden, outside toilet, scullery, kitchen, front room and bedrooms

104 *overleaf* In 1858 William Cafferata bought Beacon Hill quarry from the Newark Plaster Company, extending his operations to Hawton quarry later in the century. The safety of the forty-foot high cat-walks was not questioned until after the First World War. Surprisingly, the only man to fall, with a full load, escaped with a sprained ankle

105 A row of lime kilns in a quarry at Mansfield Woodhouse. The opening at the foot of the wall marks the bottom of the kiln, where the fire is lit. The smoke can be seen escaping from the top of the kiln, through the earth which seals in the layers of limestone and coal. The lime was sold for use on farms and in builders' mortar

106 Cropwell Bishop wharf on the Grantham canal where gypsum for use in the lace dressing industry and white plaster for surgical bandages is loaded onto barges belonging to the Snaith Plaster and Cement company and to Richard Furley & Co. of Gainsborough. *c.*1910

107 This fleet of delivery vans belonged to the Home Brewery Company of Daybrook. The clear water from the company's wells was naturally rich in the salts needed for the brewing process. The company celebrates its centenary in 1977

108 By 1905 the Daybrook Laundry,
established by the Robinson brothers in
the 1870s, had over 30 delivery vans.
These were backed into the building
where the baskets were unloaded

109 Large articles were pressed over heated rollers but smaller items were ironed by hand by one of the 150 girls employed for this purpose

110 The women in the sorting rooms divided the loads into tablecloths, shirts, collars, coloured articles and woollen clothes which were then passed to the washhouses

111 In fine weather most of the washing was hung outside in extensive drying grounds but in wet weather heated air was forced through large rooms filled with rows of wet clothes

112 John Watson moved his boat building firm to Beckingham in 1888, employing about 50 men and constructing craft up to one thousand tons. The narrow-gauge railway was used to edge the boats on rollers towards the River Trent for launching at high tide. Later this boat was dismantled and shipped to Berbice, British Guiana, where the numbered pieces were reassembled by native labour

113 In William Kiddier's workshop in Sneinton Street, Nottingham in 1902, journeymen and apprentices can be seen making various sorts of brushes by hand. The table on the right holds white-washing brushes, in the centre the panhand sets bristles or 'hairs' into a broom stock and on the table on the left bristles await 'sorting' into colours and 'dragging' into sizes

114 F. G. Connock, M. Irving, M. Ross Browne and H. Belcher outside the Humber motor works at Beeston in July 1903. The Nottingham Automobile Club was there at the invitation of Mr Belcher, who was an agent for Humber cars and drove them in hill climbs organised by the Club

115 Harvey Foster of Sheffield poses in his 50 horse-power racing Wolseley outside the Nottingham motor mart in 1903. Sir Albert R. Atkey may have been the first to introduce the internal combustion engine to the town when he drove over Trent Bridge in the summer of 1897. The car was a De Dion and Alderman Atkey later became an agent for this firm and also for Fiat, Ford, Standard and Renault

116 John Pogson, a joiner and wheelwright of Farnsfield and Blidworth, in the yard of his carriage works. Among other vehicles he is working on a delivery van for William Dowse, a governess cart, a gig and two private carriages

117 Clark's of Retford expanded their dyeing business in 1894 to include a steam laundry. A. B. Clark invented a dry cleaning process whereby clothes were immersed in a cement cistern fitted with benzine. After the benzine evaporated the clothes were ironed and pressed. The success of the process ensured that dry cleaning became the more important side of the business and the dyeworks moved out to Hallcroft in 1904 while the laundry occupied the whole of the original premises in Grove Street

118 Thomas Humber began business in Nottingham in 1868. He made his first bicycle in 1871 in a workshop in Stretton Street. This machine is a Humber tandem tricycle of 1888. The riders sat each side of the axle – the heavier on the back

MARKETS AND FAIRS

119 Mansfield's corn and provision markets were held every Thursday and Saturday. In 1839 a row of shops was removed from the centre of the Market Place and ten years later the memorial to Lord George Bentinck, M.P. was erected in their place. Designed by Thomas Chambers Hine, it cost £1500 which had been raised by a county subscription

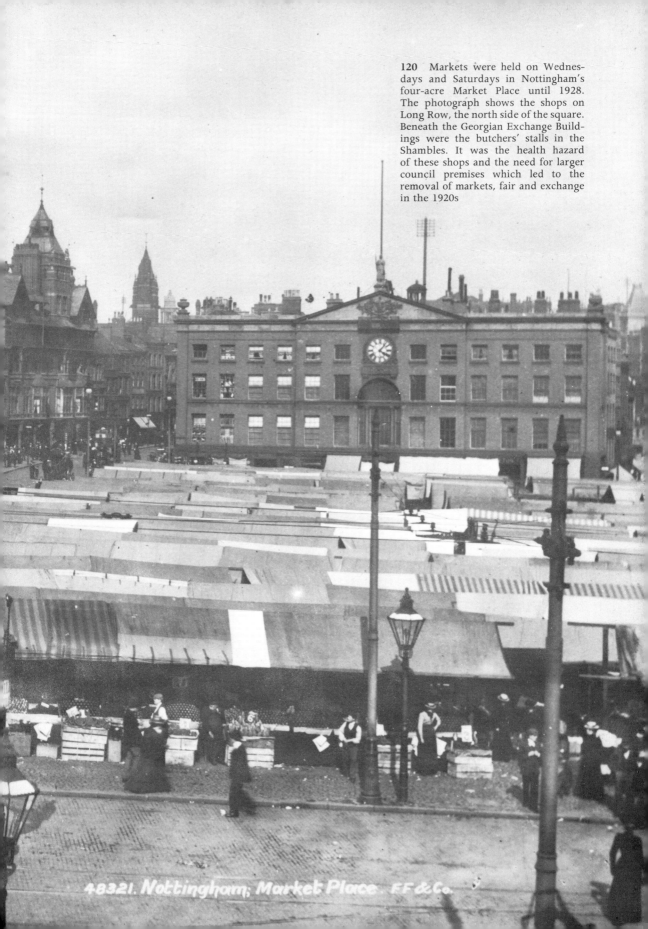

120 Markets were held on Wednesdays and Saturdays in Nottingham's four-acre Market Place until 1928. The photograph shows the shops on Long Row, the north side of the square. Beneath the Georgian Exchange Buildings were the butchers' stalls in the Shambles. It was the health hazard of these shops and the need for larger council premises which led to the removal of markets, fair and exchange in the 1920s

48321. Nottingham; Market Place. F.F & Co.

121 Newark cattle market was originally held in the grounds of the Castle. The new market was opened on 20 April 1886 by the Cattle Market Company with a capital of £6000. Tolls on animals offered for sale ranged from 2d for a pig to 2/6d for a stallion. Those selling hay, straw, fodder or roots in wagons were charged 2/-, in carts only 1/-

122 This view of Newark Market Place was taken in 1906 by Francis Frith. The tower of St Mary Magdalene, the parish church, rises over the Central printing works, the offices of Jesse Stennett, proprietor of the Newark Herald, published each Saturday. Other premises shown are those of Job Dennis, rope and twine manufacturer and Friend's music warehouse

123 Nottingham's St Matthews Fair, which provided an important venue for marketing livestock, foodstuffs and general wares, was first mentioned in 1284. Known as Goose Fair since the sixteenth century, it was held in the Market Place and surrounding streets until 1927. Entertainments have always been present, but roundabouts only appeared about 1870 when easier transport of goods made the trading aspect of the fair less important

124 This photograph by George Mills shows the preparations for the Newark fair in 1903. Six fairs were held annually in the town mainly for horses, cattle, sheep and pigs

TRADESPEOPLE

125 Mr William Hallam, greengrocer
and fishmonger of Church Street, Ruddington, wheels his barrow through
High Street *c.*1905. The butcher's shop
is closed for the summer and the bank
only opened from 11 a.m. to 2 p.m.
each Tuesday and Friday

126 Sausages decorate the window of Thomas Watson Ward's shop at 176, Victoria Road, Kirkby-in-Ashfield, whose population he served from 1895 to 1920

127 Fashionable ladies shopped in the main towns of the county for clothes. George Hutton, in his fur warehouse on Pelham Street, Nottingham, was supplying mink marmot necklets at 20/6 with muffs to match at 18/9. A seal coat cost £20, but a bargain in his sale was a golf cape with reversible lining at 21/-. *c.*1902

128 Hannah Stevenson stands at the door of her shop in Church Street, Ruddington *c.*1900. She tried the trades of fishmonger, coal dealer and carrier before settling in a general store. The site is now occupied by the Co-operative Stores

129 The Household Stores at the bottom of Robinson's yard, Front Street, Arnold stood near the site of the present Washeteria. The sign outside the door is advertising Sunlight lamp oil

130 *overleaf* The small market town of Bingham in the Vale of Belvoir had a population of 1500 in 1893 when the photograph was taken. Frederick Castledine and his family had been selling and delivering ham, bacon, groceries and bread in the town for five years

131 Hucknall Co-operative's central store in the Market Place was opened by Mr John Collins on 24 September 1898. The building, at a cost of £6000, provided a general store on the ground floor, general offices, board room, strong room and an assembly hall to accommodate 450 people on the upper floors

LEISURE ACTIVITIES

132 This procession of one of the county's many Freemason's Lodges is walking gaily along Main Street, Sutton Bonington. The King's Head Inn can be seen in the background

133 Notts. County Football Club, the oldest League Club in the country, was founded in 1862. This photograph shows the last game played on Trent Bridge Cricket ground (between County and Aston Villa on 16 April, 1910) before the move to Meadow Lane later that year. County lost 2–3

134 The Nottinghamshire Golf Club was established in 1887 and moved to the course in Bulwell Forest one year later. As the sport grew more popular more facilities were needed and this gentleman is inaugurating the course at Bulwell Hall in 1910

136 The team of the First Test Match against Australia 1899, played at Trent Bridge. Left to right: standing, Titmarsh (umpire), G. H. Hirst, T. Hayward, W. Gunn, J. T. Hearne, W. Storer, W. Brockwell (reserve), Barlow (umpire); seated, C. B. Fry, Prince Ranjitsinhji, W. G. Grace (captain), F. S. Jackson; at front, W. Rhodes, J. T. Tyldesley. This was W. G. Grace's last test match and ended in a draw

135 This tug-of-war took place at a garden party at Welbeck Abbey in 1899. The photograph is one of a series taken by Joseph Byron of New York

137 The Newark Bowling Club laid out the green on London Road in 1809 behind the Crown and Falcon Inn. For over one hundred years of its existence the Club team never lost on home ground

138 The first Sutton men to distinguish themselves in glee singing between 1830 and 1860 were George Brooks, composer, conductor and alto, Herbert Taylor, tenor, John Bartholmew Handley, tenor robusto, and John Turner, bass

139 The Hayward choir and accompanists pose outside the Great Northern Station house on Linby Lane, Hucknall in 1890. Mr William Hayward was station-master – his son Douglas holds the baton

140 When this photograph of Scott and Limb and the Denman's Head bands was taken in Sutton Market place in 1864, the town boasted six brass bands. The names of the musicians are R. Scott, conductor of Scott & Limb's, J. Handley, E. Dennis, S. Cauldwell, H. Oscroft, E. Handley, S. Hall, W. Green, A. Caunt, J. Naylor, W. Bryan, G. Scott, S. Oldham, J. Searson, E. Limb and J. Dennis, conductor of Denman's Head

141 Scene painting for a production by the Mansfield Amateur Dramatic Club in the 1890s. The secretary was John Harrop White, town clerk and an important citizen of Mansfield

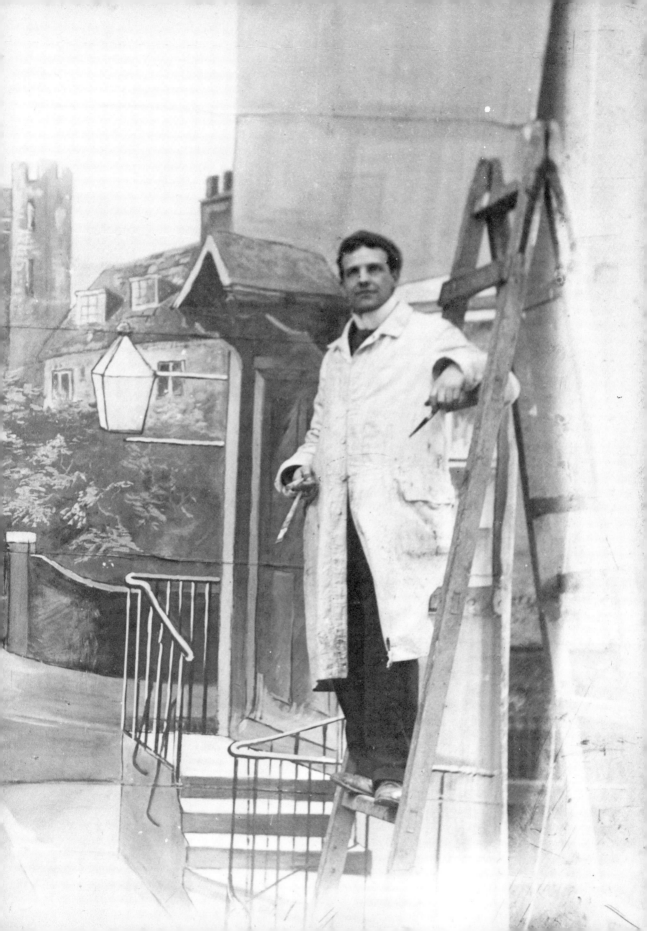

2 The Nottinghamshire Bicycle Club first promoted a one mile championship race on Trent Bridge cricket ground in 1870. By 1903, when these ladies took part, the social and touring activities were more popular than rac—

143 During the May Day celebrations at Hucknall the children gather outside the town library erected in 1888 by J. Ellis and H. Paget, proprietors of the local pit. One of the banners proclaims 'God bless our colliery lads'

144 The Golden Ball hotel in Victoria Square, Worksop was owned by William Wheeler in 1900. This photograph shows the dining room and staff

145 The whole of the county cele-
brated the Coronation of King Edward
VII on 9 August 1902. Bingham market
place is the setting for this patriotic
procession

146 Outdoor parties were commonly
held throughout the county on special
occasions. This photograph may show
the staff, patients and their families of
the Medical Hospital Home at Mansfield
Woodhouse

147 One of the county's best known public houses was the Trent Bridge Inn, West Bridgford. William Clarke, the proprietor from 1837 to 1846, enclosed the field behind the inn to form the Trent Bridge Cricket Ground. The present building dates from 1885

148   James Warner is making a delivery to the Parliament Oak on Church Street, Mansfield Woodhouse in 1890. The licensee at the time was William Spibey